THE FUTURE
CONSERVATISM

The Gregynog Papers

Volume Three • Number Two

Jonathan Evans MEP

Welsh Academic Press
Cardiff

Published in Wales by Welsh Academic Press,
an imprint of

Ashley Drake Publishing Ltd
PO Box 733
Cardiff
CF14 2YX
www.ashleydrake.com

First Impression – April 2002

ISBN
1 86057 0658

British Library Cataloguing-in-Publication Data.
A CIP catalogue for this book is available from the
British Library.

THE AUTHOR

Jonathan Evans is leader of the Conservatives in the European Parliament and has been a member of the European Parliament for Wales since 1999. He is a former MP for Brecon and Radnor (1992-97) and served as Under Secretary of State for Wales in the last Conservative Government. He has also served as a government minister at the DTI and the Lord Chancellor's Dept. He is a former deputy chairman of Tai Cymru (Housing for Wales). He is a solicitor by profession, and was managing partner of a major Cardiff law firm before entering Parliament.

The Institute of Welsh Affairs exists to promote quality research and informed debate affecting the cultural, social, political and economic well-being of Wales. IWA is an independent organisation owing no allegiance to any political or economic interest group. Our only interest is in seeing Wales flourish as a country in which to work and live. We are funded by a range of organisations and individuals. For more information about the Institute, its publications, and how to join, either as an individual or corporate supporter, contact:

IWA - Institute of Welsh Affairs
Ty Oldfield
Llantrisant Road
Llandaf
Cardiff
CF5 2YQ

Tel 029 2057 5511
Fax 029 2057 5701
Email wales@iwa.org.uk
Web www.iwa.org.uk

PREVIOUS GREGYNOG PAPERS

Creating an Entrepreneurial Wales by Dylan Jones-Evans (2001)
Our Welsh Heritage by Richard Keen (2000)
Devolution: A Process Not an Event by Ron Davies MP (1999)
State of the Arts by David Clarke (1998)
The Welsh Image by John Smith MP (1998)
NHS Wales: Business or Public Service? by Professor David Cohen (1997)
Lessons from the Sea Empress by Neil Caldwell and Clive Morgan (1997)
The Place of North Wales by Huw Vaughan Thomas (1996)

The IWA wishes to thank the
Gwendoline and Margaret Davies Charity
for their support with the publication of this book

CONTENTS

Preface

With the second election to the National Assembly little more than a year away, this is a timely moment to consider the future of the Welsh Conservative Party. In the past it has adopted a position on the edge of Welsh politics. This has certainly been the case geographically, with its electoral strongholds being at the Welsh periphery in such constituencies as Monmouth, Pembrokeshire and Clwyd West. In policy terms it has applied as well, with Labour, Liberal Democrats and Plaid Cymru sharing a good deal in common so far as social issues are concerned in contradistinction to the Conservatives. In the 1997 devolution referendum the Conservatives were the only party that campaigned for a No vote.

However, as this paper makes clear, the coming of the National Assembly has radically changed this position. As a result of proportional representation and the operation of the regional list Conservatives now represent every corner of Wales. Furthermore, while many policy differences still remain, they have now accepted devolution and have announced that they wish to contribute to the success of the National Assembly. In these circumstances the future of Welsh Conservatism should be of concern to all involved in Welsh politics.

There are two further reasons. The proportional system operating in Welsh elections means that coalition arrangements in the Assembly are likely to be the norm. As Welsh Conservatives increasingly adopt a specifically Welsh agenda, so the possibility of their participating in some future coalition becomes more feasible. Secondly, in the natural course of events, sooner or later we will see the return of a Conservative Government at Westminster. In those circumstances the role of Welsh

Conservatives in the National Assembly will be critical to Wales.

This is the eighth paper that has arisen out of a seminar held at Gregynog and been published by the Institute in association with the University of Wales Conference Centre near Newtown, Powys. Each seminar comprises around ten people including the author and the two editors. They meet for dinner and an opening presentation by the author during a weekend evening and stay overnight. The seminar then continues the following day.

The seminar out of which this paper has been produced was held in July 1999. The reason for the delay in publication has been the continuing problems that have beset the Conservative leadership in the National Assembly, combined with the onset of the 2001 UK general election. The author felt he should wait until some stability had been achieved before coming to a settled view of his own. Those attending the seminar were Robert Buckland, a barrister who has been a Conservative Parliamentary and Assembly candidate; the historian, Dr. John Davies; Glyn Davies, the Conservative AM for Mid and West Wales; Martyn Holland, a banking executive and former chairman of the Welsh Young Conservatives; David Melding, the Conservative AM for South Wales Central; and Gareth Neale, a former college lecturer who is a Conservative councillor on Cardiff County Council.

All contributed extensively to the discussions. However, the contents of this published paper are the responsibility of the author alone.

John Osmond
Director
Institute of Welsh Affairs
March 2002

INTRODUCTION

With the advent of the National Assembly a fundamental question faces Welsh Conservatives. As the standard bearers of centre right politics, how can we carve out a new agenda directly relevant to the specific needs of Wales, while remaining true to our fundamental British unionist roots and ideals?

The IWA first invited me to consider this issue in June 1999, shortly after the European elections and the first elections to the new Assembly. Welsh Conservatives had just recorded their worst ever electoral performance. We languished in the opinion polls, with commentators writing off our chances of ever again forming a Westminster Government.

Much has changed in Welsh politics since then but much remains unchanged. We have seen the fall of Ron Davies, Alun Michael and Rod Richards; tumult in the Labour Group; a Labour/Liberal Democrat coalition in the National Assembly; the sidelining of Mike German pending police and European audit inquiries relating to his former employment; turmoil in the Plaid Cymru group with the pending retirement of its three heavyweight AMs, Dafydd Wigley, Cynog Dafis and Phil Williams and the painfully lightweight Plaid leadership of Ieuan Wyn Jones.

In the meantime, the National Assembly government under the eccentric direction of Rhodri Morgan daily fails to match the aspirations of those who voted for it. It is an administration that is obsessed with names and titles. The chumminess of its inclusive "first names only" set-up hardly disguised a vicious first year in which Christine, Alun, Tom, Peter and Rosemary successively perished. Thereafter, there came the elevation from "Secretaries" to

"Ministers" and of the "First Secretary" to "First Minister" and finally the baptism of "Welsh Assembly Government".

Posturing over how AMs are addressed has equally been matched by posturing over their "courageous" decision to pour millions of pounds into commissioning a new Assembly building to match the self-importance of our new national governors.

If Conservatives believed any of this would make an impact on the polls in Wales, they were to be sadly disappointed in the 2001 General Election. While recording a marginal improvement in their share of the vote to more than 20 per cent, the Conservatives failed to win a parliamentary seat in Wales for a second successive General Election.

RE-POSITIONING THE WELSH CENTRE RIGHT

So, the past two years have produced a much changed political landscape but in the end the challenges that Welsh Conservatives face remain similar. The Tories' traditional political strength in being rightly and proudly identified with Britain and the Union seems consistently to cloud our ability to be seen in Wales as a party that puts Wales and Welsh interests first. This is the likeliest explanation of those opinion polls which record a disparity in intention to vote Conservative in Westminster and National Assembly elections.

Throughout the 20th century Conservative activists in Wales have struggled with this apparent contradiction. At one stage the Party even entitled itself "The Conservative Party **in** Wales" and, for administrative convenience, meetings of its Welsh Council were held in Ludlow, Shropshire.

Throughout our history, Welsh Conservatives have remained a minority party. Our electoral fortunes have risen to some extent at times of particular UK success for the party but at times of political difficulty Welsh Conservatives have come close to parliamentary wipe-out. In 1929, only one Conservative MP was elected and representation was down to three in the elections of 1945, 1950, 1951 and 1966.

During a century in which the UK Conservative Party has achieved greater electoral success than any other political party in western Europe Welsh voters have not only bucked the UK trend – they have consistently bucked the European trend as well. There is almost no country in Europe where the centre right has secured as little success as the Conservative Party in Wales.

What do I mean by the politics of the centre right? All political decisions involve striking some form of balance. The Conservative position places us on the centre right in balancing the roles of the private and public sectors, of individual personal freedom against collective responsibility, of personal obligation against central authority, of the increasing diversity of personal lifestyles against the need for stability in childhood and of the need for business competitiveness measured against the requirements of sustainable development and corporate responsibility.

In the new politics of Wales we need to analyse honestly why this centre right perspective has been so weak and to consider how the political agenda of those of us on the centre right can be fully incorporated at all levels into Welsh politics. Conservatives need to seriously consider these issues. Other parties also need to examine whether 'inclusive' politics go beyond merely agreeing with Labour in the National Assembly and embrace the sort of ideas put forward recently by the editor of *Barn*, Simon Brooks[1], recognising that Welsh politics in the twenty first century must not continue to slander and demonise Conservatism and the politics of the centre-right, as it so successfully had done in the twentieth.

Tony Blair had to change the name of the Labour Party in order to make the party electable in the southern part of England after so many negative images of Labour had been left in the public's mind from the events of the late 1970s. However, the baggage of history that Welsh Conservatives have to carry goes back almost a century beyond this. No doubt the industrial history of Wales, the political division between capital and labour, the rise of the Labour Party from Welsh roots, and the later wholesale economic dependence on the state-owned industries of coal and steel are the bedrock of this antipathy.

The late Professor Gwyn Williams wrote of the "*unholy trinity of Toryism – the baron, the bishop and the brewer"* as the *"enemies of the Welsh nation".*[2] When Jim Callaghan's despised government was defeated in a vote of confidence in March 1979, Plaid Cymru's members voted for the Labour Government, while the Scottish Nationalists were happy to vote with the Tories. Plaid's action was described by Labour historian (and recently ennobled) Professor Kenneth Morgan as demonstrating *"the traditional reluctance of spokesmen for Welsh sentiment to return any Tory government to power".* Indeed, Kenneth Morgan interpreted the Conservatives' improved performance in Wales in that election as an example of Wales becoming *"less Welsh".*[3]

It is also frequently deeply frustrating for those who espouse and promote the political values of the centre right to find that the first response of our political opponents is to churn up supposed events from sixty to a hundred years earlier in the industrial history of Wales. Frequently, such events also bear no historical accuracy. Virtually every Tory canvassing for a vote in the valleys of South Wales will have heard of the occasion when Tory Home Secretary, Winston Churchill, allegedly ordered troops to shoot at unarmed miners in Tonypandy. Of course, we know that no such things ever occurred – and in any event Churchill at the time was Home Secretary in a **Liberal** government. However, this image of Tory oppression continues to run deep. It corrodes the opportunity for real or meaningful debate on the issues that are relevant today.

Nevertheless, when parties are in electoral difficulty on the issues, folklore remains a weapon in the armoury. During the 1999 local government and Assembly elections, in which Wayne David was defeated in the Rhondda, one Plaid Cymru candidate complained to me that Labour canvassers were desperately urging elderly voters to stick with Labour and *"vote against the Tories for what Churchill did at Tonypandy".* My biggest plea is for political opponents to recognise the mainstream role of centre right politics in the new Welsh political scene. Failing that, we Conservatives need a better knowledge of Welsh political history and some of the positive contributions we have made.

While Welsh Conservatives have no distinct and separate history, we have had many worthwhile influences on Welsh and wider British politics. It is for instance undeniable that in the latter part of the 1800s, Conservatives played their part in promoting a distinct, well received and sensitive approach to the development of state education in Wales, the lessons of which later informed change within England. The roots of state education can, therefore, be said to have been laid here – and in part by Conservatives.

Conservatives have also done more than any other Government to secure the future of the Welsh language. It is astonishing to note how many Welsh people are prepared to acknowledge this – *but only in private*. The Conservatives set up S4C, promoted Welsh language education in schools, and took the Welsh Language Act through Parliament.

Welsh Conservatives have had their influence on political institutions as well. A little known contribution was that of the Conservative victory in the 1922 by-election in Newport, which directly led to the collapse of Lloyd George's government and his defeat in the succeeding general election. On the day following the Conservative victory in Newport, Conservative Members of Parliament gathered at the Carlton Club in London and voted to break the coalition. Today, the backbench group of Conservative members at Westminster is titled the 1922 Committee in honour of the Newport victory but this is not an event that is considered by most Welsh historians to be even worthy of record.

Welsh Conservative politicians have also contributed to the success of the British party, particularly in the post-war years. Many of the most important recent figures in British politics have been Welshmen – Michael Heseltine, the former Deputy Prime Minister; Geoffrey Howe as Foreign Secretary and Kenneth Baker as Home Secretary. In more recent years Welshmen have been better represented at Cabinet level in the Conservative Party than has been the case with Labour but, for reasons that I shall develop later, this has done nothing to counter the widespread image in Wales of the Conservative Party as a centralised English force.

Notes

1. In a lecture at the National Eisteddfod, Ynys Mon, August 2000.
2. Gwyn A. Williams, *When was Wales?*, Pelican 1975. Page 217.
3. Kenneth O. Morgan, *Wales: Rebirth of a Nation 1880–1980*, Oxford University Press, 1981, page 406.

THE ROAD TO A
TORY-FREE WALES

The Conservative Party vote in Wales was remarkably consistent during the period 1970 to 1992. Although during that time the number of MPs elected to Westminster varied between six and fourteen, the proportionate share of the Conservative vote had consistently approached 30 per cent. The only occasion when this pattern was broken was in October 1974 when the Tory vote fell below 25 per cent, although this did not lead to any fall in the number of Welsh Conservative MPs. A similar consistency can be seen in the Labour Party vote which, save in 1983, has always exceeded 45 per cent of the turnout.

The consistency in the Conservative vote was particularly evident between 1979 and 1992 and mirrored the party's British election performance. Yet, the very consistency of these results obscured big shifts which have been taking place throughout the last twenty years in local government elections and by-elections.

The period of Conservative government from 1979 to 1997 saw a virtual elimination of the Conservative presence in local government in Wales. Marie Jones retired in 1999 undefeated after more than twenty years service on the Blaenau Gwent authority as that council's sole Conservative representative. At the time of her first election victory, she had been one of an army of Welsh Conservative councillors. While the Conservatives always struggled to secure significant representation on the Valley authorities, they could genuinely aspire to control Cardiff, Newport and Swansea and areas from Monmouth and the Vale of Glamorgan to Conwy and Colwyn were regarded as safe local government territory.

This pattern changed beyond recognition over the last twenty years of the 20th century. In 1995, when Marie Jones was re- elected to Blaenau Gwent, the Conservatives suffered the indignity of having just one councillor on each of the Cardiff, Newport and Swansea authorities. This significant decline in Conservative local government representation was certainly mirrored throughout the UK. In Wales, however, the party started from a significantly lower base before sinking to a position in 1995 when barely forty Conservative councillors remained.

In comparison, the Liberal Democrats and Plaid Cymru have shown that success at local government level can provide the foundations for matching success in national elections. It should have been clearer to the Conservative Party that the disappearance of our local government base would be the forerunner of an even greater disaster in national elections. It is not at all clear, however, that the Conservative Party recognised this. The sheer consistency of the Conservative vote in successive general elections appeared to endorse this complacency.

Hence, whilst Tory success in national elections was being bought against the background of continued mid-term decline in local government representation, it also contributed to an increasing centralisation in both the organisation and thinking of the Party. This trend accelerated as our local government losses mounted.

The Conservative government had also rightly made a virtue of tackling the excesses of "loony Labour councils". In many cases, Conservative policy towards local government was a proper response to the concerns raised by apparently powerless individuals and businesses whose futures were being blighted by the excesses of such councils. Nevertheless, the measures taken in order to constrain the worse excesses of the Militant Tendency robbed the Conservative Party of one of its most potent electoral weapons.

Control of individual local councils had frequently shifted on the basis of decisions made concerning the level of local government spending and the implications of this in terms of local tax rates. The constraint imposed on local councils by the "capping" regime stripped Labour local authorities of this responsibility. At a stroke, Labour local authorities appeared to become more responsible in the eyes of the public and the central Conservative government became the convenient and self-appointed scapegoat for any shortfalls in the provision of local services. Hence the Conservative Party ceased to be the party of local government representation and came to be seen more and more as the party of Westminster government.

Running in tandem with these changes came an expansion in the number and variety of public bodies created by central government in order to deliver local services. Again, in many instances, this was a proper response to the concerns of local voters about the inefficiency and poor management in the delivery of a range of local services by councils. Many of the changes introduced by the Conservative government in the 1980s regarding the provision of such services have endured despite the change of government in 1997. It is, therefore, arguable that these changes were indeed generated with a view to improving the efficiency of the delivery of public services rather than removing them from the political control of the government's opponents.

What cannot be challenged is that the strong public *perception* was of a Conservative government whose presence on local councils had fallen away, continuing to exercise control over local services through a proliferation of new public bodies, the membership of which was predominantly drawn from those sympathetic to the Conservative cause. Unfair as this may be, it was undoubtedly an image which took root in the minds of the Welsh voters.

When the Conservatives were elected to office in 1979, no fewer than eleven Conservative MPs were returned from Wales. The number rose to fourteen in 1983 and there were, accordingly, no shortage of capable candidates to fill the ministerial vacancies.

As we have seen, the overall proportion of the votes secured by the Conservatives between the late 1970s and early 1990s remained broadly consistent, falling slightly from 32.2 per cent in 1979 to 28.6 per cent in 1992. Yet, the number of Members of Parliament elected rose from 11 in 1979 to 14 in 1983 and then fell to eight in 1987 and to just six in 1992, four of whom, including myself, were new members. It is logical, and undoubtedly intellectually defensible, that ministerial responsibilities are decided solely on the basis of political experience and individual merit. Hence Conservative Prime Ministers have adopted the stance that a Cabinet is first selected before the allocation of individual ministerial responsibilities.

Logical and reasonable as this may appear, its practical outcome in Wales has further promoted the image of a centralised Westminster-based Conservative Party. Following the retirement of Nicholas Edwards (Lord Crickhowell) as Secretary of State for Wales in 1987, this process led to the appointment of a succession of able English politicians as secretaries of state. No one can seriously deny that each of the Welsh secretaries – Peter Walker, David Hunt, John Redwood and William Hague – in turn, exercised significant political influence in Cabinet. Undoubtedly, they were bigger hitters on the UK stage than any of the Labour Welsh Secretaries of State. Nevertheless, it is similarly unchallengeable that none were appointed on the basis of their knowledge or experience of Wales. Peter Walker would often remark that on a clear day Wales was visible from his Worcester constituency and when the Welsh-born David Hunt expressed his thanks to Mrs. Thatcher for the honour of being appointed Welsh secretary she clearly considered his Welshness to be an extraordinary coincidence. Most, if not all, of the Tory Welsh secretaries are regarded as having performed their role with skill and sensitivity. However, at best their tenure was portrayed as a form of "benevolent dictatorship" and the label of "Governor-General" with its colonial implications sadly attached itself to each of them.

One of the Welsh secretaries least interested in promoting the benevolent image was John Redwood. Though there is no denying John's political skills and ambition, his tenure at the Welsh Office did little to enhance the political popularity of the Conservative Party. The debate on the reform of Welsh local government provides a telling example of this negative imagery. There is no doubt that the structure of local government in Wales required revision and a return to the concept of unitary authorities based upon the traditional Welsh counties and major Welsh conurbations. Today, John Redwood has rightly been in the vanguard of those opposing the "one size fits all" approach to the Euro and economic and monetary union. Yet, the local government reorganisation in Wales and Scotland was taken through Parliament a year in advance of its consideration in England. There, the outcome was markedly different, with a more flexible approach involving unitary authorities and two-tier authorities as part of a flexible mosaic.

No such flexibility was shown by Redwood in Wales. Instead the Conservative Government's English majority was used to drive through the secretary of state's uniform local government structure. Although there could be no possibility of local government changes affecting the parliamentary constituency boundaries in the following election, our political opponents relentlessly exploited the opportunity to claim political gerrymandering. The prevailing image, sadly again, was of an English dominated party imposing an inflexible and uniform local government structure in Wales which barely twelve months later English Tory MPs were not prepared to see imposed on their own constituencies.

This lack of sensitivity to Welsh views was further demonstrated during the passage of the Welsh Language Act. The appointment by a Tory Government of Lord Elis Thomas, the former Plaid Cymru MP, as the first chairman of the Welsh Language Board had been innovative and courageous. But when the legislation was considered in committee, the Government insisted on maintaining its majority by filling the committee with English MPs, whose interest in the legislation was minimal. The prevailing image broadcast to Wales was of the Conservative government again using its English majority to have its way on legislation which covered solely Welsh issues.

The combination of fewer and fewer local councillors, the proliferation of quangos, a succession of English secretaries of state and the English Tory parliamentary majority used to settle the detail of Welsh legislation all contributed to a strong and growing perception of the Conservative Party as focused on Westminster and insensitive to Welsh concerns. So, the 1997 general election saw the realisation of Ron Davies' aim of a Tory-free Wales. The Conservative share of the Welsh vote fell to 19.6 per cent, the lowest in the 20th century, and not a single Conservative MP was returned from Wales.

MISSING THE WELSH PERSPECTIVE

Labour moved swiftly to take advantage of its 1997 landslide by calling the referendum on the establishment of the National Assembly within weeks of the General Election result. The political commentator Andrew Rawnsley starkly spells out the Labour Government's strategy[1]. Wales was dismissed by Blair as Scotland's "small and ugly sister, with interest in the Assembly confined to the Welsh".

Much has already been written of the events that then led to the paper-thin majority achieved in the referendum vote. One of the more influential outcomes, according to Rawnsley, was that the unexpected closeness of the Welsh result entrenched a policy of caution over calling any UK referendum on Euro entry which persists to this day. It is undeniable that, notwithstanding such a shattering defeat in the general election, the Welsh Conservative Party was still able to make a significant contribution to the "No" campaign, which came within a whisker of inflicting a first major defeat on Tony Blair.

This tells us something about the resilience and determination of our core Welsh supporters but it is also arguable that it led to a mistaken Conservative strategy in the run up to the National Assembly election 19 months later in May 1999. It was perhaps unwise to classify the 550,000 "No" voters as otherwise sympathetic to the Conservative message. There is no doubt that many of those who voted "No" were Labour supporters who saw no purpose in establishing a National Assembly when the general election had already produced a change of government. It is also now clear that many of the "No" voters were Liberal

Democrats who disagreed with their own Party policy on devolution. Liberal Democrat voters showed a similar hostility to their own party's European policy during the European Parliament Elections in Wales.

Cynog Dafis, Plaid Cymru's AM for Mid and West Wales, was recently asked to reconcile the strong Welsh identification with British successes in the Olympics, with a majority of Welsh people also considering themselves to be Welsh first, rather than British. Had the Government relented and agreed to the proposed Welsh 'tick box' on the next Census forms we might have been able to put some figures on this. Cynog described this phenomenon as a 'paradox'.

Whether paradox or not, the Nationalists recognised at the outset of the Assembly election campaign that their strong identification with Wales was a strength in those elections but their nationalism was a weakness. They therefore reinvented themselves, renaming their Party as 'The Party of Wales' and expressing incredulity that anyone could really have believed that they were ever Nationalists. 'Independence' was excised from the Nationalist lexicon – although its leaders confess to still using the word in private.

The Welsh Conservatives faced the converse problem. We were identified with Britain, the Union and defence of the constitution. But how strong were these issues in the context of an election to the National Assembly for Wales? As Ken Livingstone was later to show in the London Mayoral election, people were looking instead for representatives who would 'stick up for local interests' – whether in London or Wales. Unsurprisingly, the only Welsh constituency in which we secured an outright win on this criterion was Monmouth, where no- one had any doubt that David Davies would stick up for Monmouth's interests.

Elsewhere, such weapons as we had were unused. Our campaign appeared to be run on the basis of denying or apologising for all that we had done to promote the Welsh language and culture – just at the time when those factors were most important in convincing Welsh voters that we could be trusted to stick up for Wales.

And so it proved. The first elections held to the National Assembly, followed by the European elections barely five weeks later, produced what some commentators have described as "a quiet earthquake" in Welsh politics[2]. Though the turnout in these elections proved disappointing, the share of the vote achieved by Plaid Cymru heavily exceeded the expectations of most commentators or politicians. We have always recognised that there is a strong core nationalist vote of 160,000 to 170,000. A lower overall turnout figure thus helps Plaid Cymru, as their core supporters can usually be relied upon to turn out and vote. An analysis of Plaid Cymru's numerical score in a succession of recent elections endorses this argument. However, in the National Assembly election, against a background of low turnout of 46 per cent, Plaid Cymru recorded more than 300,000 votes on the regional PR system.

The results of the Assembly and European elections have catapulted Plaid Cymru from its position as the fourth party of Wales to leadership of the opposition in the National Assembly and equality of representation with Labour in the European Parliament.

In his contribution to the Gregynog series Ron Davies outlined some of the factors that brought about disillusion among Labour supporters. Ron described local government (so long a fiefdom of Welsh Labour) and Welsh politics at Westminster as a "snakepit" of "parochialism"[3]. He alleged that strategic thinking gave way to personal rivalries, jealousies and ambition. Events have since confirmed all this in both Assembly and Westminster politics: Ron Davies' ignominious exit from the Welsh Office and later his removal from the Chair of the Assembly's economic development committee; the rise and fall of Alun

Michael; the prevailing image of personal animosities in the British Cabinet, and central control from 10 Downing Street, far exceeding anything witnessed in 18 years of Tory government.

But Plaid Cymru was to squander their historic opportunity to transform Welsh politics. The "giant" of Dafydd Wigley gave way to the "pygmy" of Ieuan Wyn Jones – an apology for a leader, who bolted from the TV studios on hearing of the loss of Ynys Môn on election night and went to ground for more than a day. Ieuan Wyn's abject conduct has been a metaphor for the crushing failure of Plaid Cymru to measure up to the responsibilities entrusted to them in the National Assembly election. Turmoil and chaos have resulted, culminating in the resignation of a number of senior figures including Dafydd Wigley's own former Chairman, Guto Bebb, who has joined the Welsh Conservatives.

Guto has described the Conservatives' constructive and democratic approach in the National Assembly as a crucial factor in his decision to join the Party. But Conservatives must recognise that our effective team in the National Assembly only secured election under the referendum approved PR system.

Having secured almost 20 per cent of the vote in the disastrous 1997 general election, in the Assembly election the Conservatives were able to win a share on the most generous assessment – that of the regional vote – of barely 16 per cent. Save for the isolated and hard-fought victory in Monmouth, the Conservatives failed to win in any Welsh constituency and our presence on the National Assembly is largely due to the operation of the proportional voting system.

As a long-standing supporter of electoral reform, I have no difficulty in welcoming this development. Under "first past the post" Welsh Conservatives have consistently been under-represented at both Westminster and in local government. Martin Linton and Mary Southcott in their book "Making Votes Count", point out that at the 1997 general election, it was the Welsh Conservatives who suffered the greatest under-representation of any political party as a result of the "first past the post system". With 20 per cent of the vote the Conservatives had no representation whatsoever[4]. No political party in any region of the UK secured a higher proportion of the vote without gaining any parliamentary representation.

The difficulty with the "first past the post" system is the regional polarisation which it brings about. Thus, predominantly Labour areas become more Labour and predominately Tory areas more Tory. This phenomenon affects parties in different ways. In predominantly Conservative areas in southern England, Martin Linton has pointed out that Labour supporters in the 1980s often saw no point in voting for candidates who had no chance of success and therefore switched to the Liberals. This gave more prominence to Liberal candidates, with Labour falling to third place and thus losing credibility. As a result, even more people abandoned the Labour Party.

When Labour politicians were interviewed on radio or TV, they were MPs from other parts of the country, speaking in the accents of those other regions and thus voters had ceased to think of Labour as a party that spoke their language or articulated their concerns. And, as Martin Linton has pointed out, the same thing happened to the Conservatives in Scotland. By falling into third place behind the SNP, when Tory politicians appeared on TV, they were almost always English and this undermined the credibility of the Scottish Tories further, thus reinforcing the trend which culminated in the elimination of Conservative Scottish representation in the Commons in May 1997.

We see these parallels in Wales. I recognise that the Party has a deep-seated and principled objection to changing the "first past the post" voting system for Westminster elections. It is, however, undeniable that even in the 1997 general election, the Conservatives were proportionally over- represented in the eastern and south-eastern areas of England from where the shadow cabinet is largely drawn. It is very easy to maintain one's principled objections, when one's principles happen to so neatly coincide with electoral self- interest.

Notes

1. Andrew Rawnsley: Servants of the People: The Inside Story of New Labour. Penguin 2001.
2. See Dafydd Trystan and Richard Wyn Jones, *A Quiet Electoral Earthquake, AGENDA* Summer 1999, IWA.
3. Ron Davies, *Devolution: A Process Not an Event*, The Gregynog Papers, Volume Two, Number Two, IWA, February 1999, page 2.
4. Martin Linton and Mary Southcott *Making Votes Count – the Case for Electoral Reform*, Profile Books, 1997. Page 39, Table 4.5.

A WELSH BRAND FOR CONSERVATIVE POLICY

Earlier in this paper I suggested that Welsh commentators should refrain from their relentless demonisation of Welsh Conservatism. It is, of course, a forlorn hope. There is a powerful anti-Conservative conspiracy within what we know as the "Taffia" – those figures in the Welsh media and academia that draw together the interests of Labour, Plaid Cymru and the Liberal Democrats. This consensus pervades the National Assembly, the universities, local councils, our public bodies, our broadcasters, our press and almost every strand of public life. Even the Archbishop of Wales felt comfortable in accepting the role of patron of the Labour Party's Aneurin Bevan foundation. Such universal antipathy towards the centre right does not exist among key opinion formers in any other major country in Western Europe.

So it is in our own hands to take on and expose and denounce this comfortable anti-Tory consensus – and we are starting to do so.

For years, the Question Time current affairs programme has undertaken regional broadcasts from Cardiff, Swansea or North Wales in which the broadcasters have invited Conservative spokesmen from London or the South East to represent the Conservative Party before a Welsh audience and against Welsh-based representatives of the other parties. Complaint after complaint to the BBC made not a jot of difference – and not one of the broadcasters or journalists in Wales was prepared to do anything to challenge such blatant unfairness. On the contrary, the "Taffia" were happy to continue having the Welsh Conservatives portrayed as an "English" party in Wales. Three years ago, we had a major breakthrough when Nigel Evans, the Swansea-born spokesman on Welsh Affairs, got a Question Time invitation only to find that Ron Davies intervened with the BBC to have Nigel's invitation withdrawn and he was replaced by John Redwood. No Welsh Conservative had an invitation from that time on, and we had no support from the BBC or the Welsh press in challenging this. Would Plaid Cymru or Labour have been treated this way?

In January, the BBC announced that Question Time was to be broadcast from Cardiff, and that they had invited Rhodri Morgan, Dafydd Wigley, Lembit Opik and Julie Kirkbride, a backbench Tory MP from Bromsgrove. We complained to the BBC. Why no Conservative from Wales? They were looking for a woman they replied. Well, don't Labour, Plaid or the Lib Dems have any women politicians, we asked? We made a formal complaint of political bias against the BBC to the Director General, Greg Dyke (another former Labour member and party donor), and after going public with our concern over blatant unfairness, the Director General was obliged to intervene and we secured the first Welsh Conservative voice on Question Time.

So we have to fight for a fair chance to put our case and fair broadcasters and journalists should be on our side in this.

But in projecting the relevance of our ideas in a Welsh context and in developing a Welsh brand to our policy we must make it clear that there is no doubt about our commitment to the maintenance of the Union of Great Britain and Northern Ireland.

But we must recognise that other than one Scots MP, the Conservative Parliamentary Party is entirely composed of English Conservative MPs. To those who would claim that this shows we are an "English Party", I would point to my own election, as the sole Welsh Conservative MEP, as Leader of the Conservatives in the European Parliament – the second largest national group of MEPs in the parliament and representing every part of the UK.

While the Conservatives need 330 MPs to win an overall majority at Westminster, a milestone on that road is
the minimum of 265 seats in England, which would give
the Conservatives a majority of English seats. Securing
this level would in itself reignite a constitutional debate.
Tony Blair's response to this prospect in early 2000 was
complacent and chilling.

> ". . . the measures needed to protect a minority are
> not always the same as the measures needed to pro-
> tect a majority. England can, if it chooses, outvote
> Scotland, Ireland and Wales at any point. English
> MPs are in an overwhelming majority in voting
> through the money for Wales and Scotland."[1]

In one way or another, the outcome of Blair's constitutional
changes will mean that at some point in the future the
missing dimension – the English dimension – will have to
be addressed. Some will argue for an English Parliament
solution – among them it seems the Welsh Nationalists,
who seem to be reinventing themselves again, this time as
British federalists. However, the Nationalists' apparent
acceptance of Wales as an integral part of the British state
should fool no one. In a joint 2001 New Year interview for
BBC News 24, Alex Salmond and Elfyn Llwyd contrasted
their approaches on the 'Independence' question. Elfyn
charmingly confirmed that he was still in favour of 'the I
word' – but only in the privacy of his own home!

If the English Parliament lobby succeeds, Welsh
Conservatives must recognise that there will be profound
implications, in which the powers of the Welsh Assembly would have to be revisited. Hence, the English Parliament is not a question for England alone, but for us in
Wales too.

Rhodri Morgan has concluded that the Assembly requires the stability of a majority administration. Others consider that the underwhelming performance of the Assembly administration is due to flaws in its structure – crucially the failure to deliver the same level of power as granted to Scotland.

Welsh Secretary Paul Murphy warned in a speech in Spain that voters want better public services rather than constitutional change[2]. I remember making similar remarks throughout Wales in the referendum campaign. Yet, Paul Murphy's remarks fail to address the key issue, which is that the constitutional settlement proposed by Labour was flawed from the outset. The structure of asymmetrical devolution contains the seeds of conflict which ultimately may threaten the cohesion of the United Kingdom. This is perhaps one reason why a majority of Scots believe that Scotland will be an independent country within the next 20 years. Pointing out that the flaws in the current constitutional settlement are unsustainable is, therefore, truly a Unionist rather than a Nationalist argument. Welsh Conservatives have no obligation to defend a constitutional structure created by Labour expediency.

We must also recall Ron Davies prescription that devolution is a process not an event[3]. Labour's reasons for granting different powers to Wales were always fatuous. Wales got the minimum powers consistent with not scaring voters into voting 'No'. Once established, it was clear that any and every failure of the Assembly administration would be portrayed neither as a failure of the body nor still less its politicians but practical evidence that the Assembly required more and more power.

Perhaps it is because of this insight that there remain a number of Welsh Conservatives who still believe that the Conservatives should commit themselves to abolition of the National Assembly. In a democratic party their views must be addressed. Current Party policy expresses its firm commitment to making the National Assembly a success.

This undoubtedly grates with a number of core Party activists who passionately believe that the referendum was unfair, the Assembly has been a failure, and that the resolution of the constitutional problem lies in the Assembly's abolition.

William Hague made it clear that he believes that policy in relation to the Assembly must be 'made in Wales'. Nick Bourne and his Assembly colleagues have made an excellent start in developing specific Welsh policy themes, relevant to the powers of the Assembly yet consistent with Conservative principles. We have seen these taken forward in the fields of education, health and countryside policy, and more recently with fresh policy ideas on culture and the arts.

I am convinced that, if policy had been made in Wales in the past, we would at the very least have seen a different structure of Welsh local government, and it is also unlikely that we in Wales would have taken forward the last Conservative Government's nursery voucher programme which generated so much anti-Conservative hostility.

At the same time, we need to encourage the widest possible participation in the development of such policy. We need to create mechanisms that allow for our supporters' views to be expressed and lead to a full dialogue and a democratic outcome. And then we are entitled to expect agreement on a uniform policy, without the destructive, unattributable briefings that have recently become such a negative feature of Welsh politics.

Some other innovative steps have already been taken by the Welsh Conservative Party Board. A series of policy forums have been organised to allow members to contribute to the policy process. Party chairman, Henri Lloyd Davies and Assembly leader, Nick Bourne are also taking forward an initiative to establish a new specialist think tank under the chairmanship of one of Wales' best known economic policymakers, drawing together leading centre right academics and other senior Welsh figures to take forward new policy agendas. This is a development I wholeheartedly endorse. It will help to develop a distinctive Welsh agenda of policy thinking within a centre right context.

Notes

1. Tony Blair, speech on Britishness, London, March 28, 2000.
2. Paul Murphy, Speech to the Regional Government and Devolution Conference, Valencia, Spain. October 31, 2000, quoted in *Coaltion Politics come to Wales: Monitoring the National Assembly September to December 2000, IWA*, December 2000.
3. Ron Davies, *op. cit.*

NECESSARY NEW INITIATIVES

At the outset of the 21st century we must recognise Welsh prosperity is compromised by the continuing hostility of elements of our society to centre right politics. Wales is unique in Europe in this irrational exclusion of the Conservative perspective from the development of mature political debate. I believe major changes are required in the structure, policy and approach of the party if we are to make the most of the opportunities that lie ahead. Too often the Conservative Party had fallen into the trap of believing that all of its problems would be resolved by "better presentation".

1. The Welsh Party Leadership

Against this background, it is also essential that distinctive Welsh perspectives are fully represented in the highest levels of the party. This will be especially important when the party is in government at Westminster. In this context it has to be acknowledged that since the 1997 general election the Conservative Party has struggled to come to terms with our lack of Welsh representation in the House of Commons.

I remain at a loss in trying to understand William Hague's reasoning in addressing this weakness. The creation of a new post of constitutional affairs spokesman, with a junior spokesman for Wales, was interpreted by Welsh Conservatives as a demotion of the status of Wales in shadow cabinet decision- making. This impression was strengthened by the bizarre handling of the shadow cabinet reshuffle, which saw Nigel Evans appointed as a vice-chairman of the party with responsibility for Wales. Constitutional change has increased not diminished the need for an effective Welsh presence in the Cabinet and at all Cabinet committees. Iain Duncan Smith appears to have seen all this far more clearly than Hague. He appointed Nigel Evans as Shadow Welsh Secretary, thus clarifying the issue of political leadership in the Welsh party, while also appointing both Nick Bourne and myself to the shadow cabinet in order to participate in cabinet discussions in our own areas of responsibility. Under Hague, Wales had no voice in cabinet, whereas with Iain Duncan Smith, we have three.

2. Building European Links

I believe that it is also important that we should be building links between the Welsh party and Europe. Peter Walker initiated these links when he was Welsh secretary and undoubtedly played a key role in promoting a better understanding of Wales throughout the EU and beyond. His initiative to create links with Lombardy, Catalunya, Rhone-Alpes and Baden-Wurttemberg not only advanced the economic interests of Wales but also led to a new Welsh self-confidence in many in the industrial sector in their international business.

The Conservative Party's stance on economic and monetary union should not lead us to squander the opportunity for closer dialogue with other centre right parties throughout the European Union. We are the leading party in the European Democratic Union, which is a magnet for many of the new centre right democratic parties in central and eastern Europe that will be joining the EU in 2004. Our political allies are currently in government in more than half of Europe and may shortly be in government again in Germany.

Iain Duncan Smith has made it clear that his strong interest in examining European solutions for the more effective delivery of public services requires us to get out and meet centre right political allies. Welsh Conservatives have had many meetings over the past eighteen months with members of the European Parliament from other EU countries who share our centre right political values – people like Ari Vatanen, the former World Motor Rally champion from Finland, General Morillon from France, who commanded Nato forces in Bosnia, and Dana Scallon, the Independent MEP from Ireland and many others. These meetings have not only helped us to identify the range of issues where we share a common approach – as well as a number where we disagree – but have also helped us to see our allies at the centre of mainstream political activity in their countries.

We must also learn from our political allies in Spain. Our centre right allies in the Partido Popular either control or participate in the regional governments in Galicia and Catalunya, often quoted by Welsh nationalists as models of successful regional government. These regions are run by centre right Conservative administrations. They appear to retain the trust and confidence of their voters while also maintaining a Spanish-level centre right government in Madrid. Similar lessons can be learnt in Baden Wurttemburg, where the Christian Democratic Union (CDU) shares many of our ideas on European issues. I hope that our team in the National Assembly and the party leadership in Wales will build on these links in order to refine our political ideas.

3. Greater Autonomy for the Welsh Party

During his leadership of the Conservative Party, William Hague introduced a wide range of reforms to central party organisation. Within Wales, changes have taken place to meet this template.

Nevertheless, further organisational changes will be required, if we are to meet the challenge of making the Conservatives the leading force in Welsh politics. Central to this project must be the organisation of the way the party is run from within Wales. Ron Davies has rightly pointed out the contradiction of Labour facilitating the transfer of powers from Westminster to Cardiff and then not exercising parallel decision-making in respect of its own party organisation.

Conservative Central Office in London appears to have adopted a somewhat ambivalent approach towards autonomy in the party structure in Wales and the English regions. For many years the party organisation was run on a regional basis with strong regional offices. As party finances have contracted and the party machine in London has grown, we have gradually seen the erosion of the Conservative Party's regional structures. I believe that we are now at the time when Central Office staff in Wales must come fully under the control and remit of the Welsh Conservative Party.

4. Selecting Women as Candidates

I have already acknowledged the quality of our National Assembly team. Yes, there is one glaring omission: the absence of any women from the Welsh Conservative Group. There was a similar omission from the Conservative Party list in the recent European Parliament elections. This situation just cannot continue.

The Party has rightly resisted moves towards positive discrimination or artificial twinning of constituencies in order to address the issue of under-representation of women. We rightly believe that merit should be the overriding criterion for selection as candidates for public office. Nevertheless, we have to recognise that this principled stance is creating an unacceptable situation for us. There are many able Welsh women who are active within the ranks of the Party. Many of them stood as candidates in the recent Assembly elections. Nevertheless, the selection procedures have failed to result in any of these women achieving election. We must urgently find ways of addressing this unacceptable situation. Perhaps we need immediately to set up a panel of prospective women candidates for Assembly, Westminster and European elections and give them the training and the opportunity to speak up for the party throughout Wales. Giving a number of women the chance to develop a high profile within our ranks may be one means of redressing the balance in favour of women, without adopting loaded shortlists.

The Welsh Conservative Party has consistently selected women for position of high influence in the party. Many of the leading figures in recent years have been women and, of course, we take pride in the great achievement of Margaret Thatcher in becoming Britain's first women Prime Minister. There can now be no doubt that Margaret Thatcher did infinitely more to promote the capability of women in all walks of public life than has been achieved by any of the one hundred or so "Blair babes" elected in the 1997 general election. We must give our women candidates in Wales a fairer deal.

5. Rebuilding our Local Roots

As I pointed out earlier, the erosion of our support in local Government was a precursor to our huge defeat in 1997. There can be no doubt, therefore, that rebuilding a base in local government at all levels is an essential step to re-establishing the Conservative Party in Wales. I would advocate a targeted approach to this.

The key message must be the need to ensure Conservative candidates stand everywhere. Of course, the independent tradition in many parts of local government in Wales runs counter to this. When I served as Member of Parliament for Brecon and Radnor, the Radnorshire District Council was an independently controlled authority. I calculated that although there was only one official Conservative on the council, the authority would be Conservative overnight if the members of the local Conservative association on the council agreed to sit as Conservatives.

However, there are many rural areas where the individual record of service of such local councillors is a more important factor to the electors than their individual allegiance. For those who claim that independence is a long-dead tradition in Wales, I would merely point to the Assembly election results in Carmarthen, Ceredigion and Powys to show that there can still be powerful independent votes, even in an Assembly election. Party labels, in my view, should not be the only consideration.

Nevertheless, we do need to re-establish our former position in the big local authorities of Cardiff, Newport, Swansea and in North Wales. The recent excellent local government results in Monmouth and the Vale of Glamorgan show what can be achieved with hard work, good candidates, unity and determination.

6. *Welsh Tories and the Media*

If we are to ensure the success of a mature new Welsh politics, the media will also have to play its part in giving a fair crack of the whip to Welsh Conservatives.

This is not just another plea for party political balance, or an attack on the media as a nest of socialist vipers.

There is a real responsibility on the part of the media to ensure that all elements of the political spectrum, including the centre right perspective of Welsh Conservatism, are properly portrayed in an inclusive Welsh politics. What do I mean by this? I have already highlighted occasions when political discussion programmes such as *Question Time* include Welsh politicians from the other political parties and then invite English politicians to represent the Tory case before a Welsh audience. Broadcasters and journalists must be aware of the impact this unfairness has. Yet, the BBC steadfastly refuses to relent.

At our annual conference in Cardiff in 2000, for instance, we had an important debate on European issues, addressed by many Welsh Conservatives. Not one word was broadcast by the BBC, even though all their broadcasters and equipment were present. Yet, the following day BBC Cymru devoted a half hour radio programme to a phone-in on Europe, with Teresa Gorman speaking from a radio studio in Essex! How can Welsh Conservatives successfully promote their Welsh identity when the dice are loaded in this way?

Welsh Tories see this as evidence of media hostility to the party. I see it as the media failing to play its role in ensuring full and mature debate in the new politics of Wales. We have similar difficulties with the Welsh newspapers. In recent years it has been hard to find any Welsh newspaper that has been anything other than hostile to the Conservative Party. It has been impossible to find one whose editorial policy is to support the party.

During European Parliamentary elections in 1999, independent monitoring of the Western Mail revealed an overwhelming disparity between coverage of Labour – and particularly Glenys Kinnock – and the other political parties. Yet, the editor of the Western Mail fiercely and angrily resists any charge of partiality.

When the Western Mail's owners, Trinity, were

endeavouring to acquire Mirror Group Newspapers, they gave a public assurance that the editorial policy of the Daily Mirror in supporting the Labour Party would never change, if they were successful. Today, most of the newspapers in Wales are in the hands of Trinity, and the publishers have successfully persuaded the Labour Government that they should be allowed this monopoly position, as they are really in the wider 'information' market. If that is true, then we must ensure that the Welsh Conservatives are more successful in promoting our ideals and policies through this new information society than we have been in persuading Welsh newspaper editors to treat us fairly.

CONCLUSION

This paper has been written at a time of major change in Welsh politics. Plaid Cymru's success in the National Assembly elections shows that many Welsh voters are prepared to re-assess their political allegiances. But, the disillusion of Labour voters with their party has proved contagious and has now infected Plaid Cymru's voters as well.

The challenge of catching this mood and encouraging Welsh voters to give Welsh Conservatives the opportunity to serve will not be easy. There is not just unreasonable entrenched hostility to the Party in some of the traditional Labour voting areas of Wales but this negativity pervades many layers of political influence in broadcasting, journalism, the arts and the academic world.

But Conservatives are fighting back. We have the most successful student movement in the Welsh universities, where young people free from the shackles of prejudice are attracted to our centre right values.

We have been at the forefront in promoting the interests of rural Wales, while the Liberals are hamstrung by their coalition with Labour and Plaid Cymru follow a European Green Party agenda that conflicts with the interest of farmers and those who earn their living in the countryside.

Our Assembly members are acknowledged as the most effective group within the National Assembly, where we have actively promoted health and education issues.

People are looking less and less at the political agendas set by the parties, but are judging politicians issue by issue. In this atmosphere, the old political prejudices based on non-conformism, radicalism and inaccurate nineteenth century industrial history can perhaps be banished to history. These prejudices have currently sustained a century of Labour local government dominance which daily fails the people of Wales.

To achieve success we need to change our thinking. While remaining unequivocally committed to the Union of Great Britain and Northern Ireland, we must work even harder to develop and embrace a specific Welsh profile. This will only happen if we bring forward a clear and distinct policy agenda that is relevant to Wales and rooted in Conservative principles. We need to show that we can always be trusted to stick up for Wales. And if we want to be trusted with power in Wales we must show that we are competent, moderate and practical in our approach.

Welsh Conservatives have suffered many reverses over the years. The next period of Welsh politics could well be our opportunity to throw off the negative baggage of history and to build a position of real relevance and influence at the centre of Welsh politics. We are here to serve the people of Wales.

PUBLICATIONS

AGENDA

The Institute's regular journal appears three times a year.
£5 for a single issue, £15 yearly subscription.

MONITORING THE NATIONAL ASSEMBLY

Coalition Creaks over Health*: Monitoring the Assembly Sept. – Dec. 2001 (Dec. 01) £10*

A Period of Destabilisation *Monitoring the Assembly May – Aug. 2001 (Aug. 01) £10*

Farming Crisis Consolidates Assembly's Role *Mar. – May 2001 (May 01) £10*

The Economy Takes Centre Stage *Monitoring the National Assembly Dec. 00 – Mar. 01 (Mar. 01) £10*

Coalition Politics Come to Wales *edited by John Osmond (Dec. 00) £10*

Devolution Looks Ahead *edited by John Osmond (Sept. 00) £10*

Devolution in Transition *edited by John Osmond (June 00) £10*

Devolution Relaunched *edited by John Osmond (March 00) £10*

Devolution: A Dynamic, Settled Process? *by John Osmond (Dec. 99) £10*

CURRENT RESEARCH REPORTS

Tools for the Learning Country *(Dec. 01) £5*

World Best Practice in Regional Economic Development
(Jun. 01) £10

The Search for Balance: Taxing & Spending across the United Kingdom *by Ross Mackay (Jun. 01) £10*

Knowledge and the Welsh Economy *by Professor Sir Adrian Webb (Jun. 01) £10*

A Guide to European Funding in Wales 2000–2006 *by Dr. Gareth Jones (May 01) £10*

Inclusive Government and Party Management: The National Assembly for Wales and the Work of its Committees *edited by J. Barry Jones and John Osmond (Mar. 01) £15*

An Icon for Modern Wales: Realising the Benefits of the National Botanic Garden *by Neil Caldwell & John Stoner (Feb. 01) £10 Main Report £20*

Craft As Art: Projecting the Makers of Wales Within the Global Economy *by John Osmond (Feb. 01) £10*

Beyond the Border: The Acceptability of the WelshBac to Higher Education Institutions outside Wales *(bilingual) by Cerian Black & John David (Sept. 00) £10*

Small Loans for Small Businesses: Developing Micro-Credit in Wales *by Dr. Nigel Blewitt (July 00) £10*

The Irish Experience of Objective One *by John Osmond (June 00) £10*

Waste in Wales – A National Resource *(ECOTEC) (Feb. 00) £30, Summary report £10*

Building a Knowledge-Driven Welsh Economy *by Gareth Jones and John Osmond (Nov. 99) £10*

Unravelling the Knot: The Interaction of UK Treasury & EU Funding for Wales *by Dr. Gillian Bristow and Dr. Nigel Blewitt (Nov. 99) £30*

The WelshBac: From Wales to the World *(Aug. 99) £5*

The National Assembly Agenda *(Nov. 98) Edited by John Osmond £10*

The Other Wales: the Case for Objective One Funding *by Adam Price and Kevin Morgan (July 98) £10*

THE GREGYNOG PAPERS

Polemical but informed policy papers by experts in the field
Creating an Entrepreneurial Wales *by Professor Dylan Jones-Evans (Sept. 01) £7.99*
Our Welsh Heritage *by Richard Keen (Feb. 00) £7.50*
Devolution: A Process Not an Event *by Ron Davies MP (Feb. 99) £7.50*

IWA DISCUSSION PAPERS

A Reorganisation Too Far: IWA Response to the National Assembly consultation document Structural Change in the NHS in Wales *by Gareth Jones (Oct. 01) £5*
Enhancing Welsh Input into Westminster Legislation *by Prof. Keith Patchett & John Osmond (Mar. 01) £5*

To order a report (there is a p&p charge of £1.50) contact: IWA, Ty Oldfield, Llantrisant Road, Llandaf, Cardiff, CF5 2YQ, Tel: 029 2057 5511, Fax: 029 2057 5701, wales@iwa.org.uk